Lovely Nightmare

Krystal Gray

Copyright © 2018 Krystal Gray

Front & Back Cover Illustrations:
Krystal Gray & Darren Faulkner

Book Illustrations: Krystal Gray

All rights reserved.

ISBN-13: 978-1-7751372-0-7

Thank You

TO MY **GRAMS** FOR ALWAYS BELIEVING IN ME. I MISS YOU DEARLY.

TO MY **UNCLE** DARREN FOR CREATING THE ILLUSTRATIONS FOR THE COVER AND BACK. I WILL ALSO MISS YOU.

TO MY **GRAMPS** AND **MOM** FOR PASSING ON THE LOVE AND TALENT OF WRITING.

TO MY **HUSBAND**, DAN, FOR BEING MY EMOTIONAL SUPPORT AND MY BIGGEST SUPPORTER AND BEST FRIEND. I LOVE YOU.

MY **BIG SIS**, LIZ, SHOWING ME THE WAY INTO THE PUBLISHING WORLD AND HELPING MAKE MY DREAM A REALITY.

MY **LITTLE SIS**, SAM, FOR BEING A SOUNDING BOARD, PROOF READING, EDITING AND GIVING ME IDEAS FOR ART WHEN MY BRAIN STOPPED WORKING.

MY **BABY SIS**, CASEY, FOR PROOF READING AND REVIEWING MY BOOK AND BEING A GREAT SUPPORT.

NOTE

As you read the contents within this book feel free to colour the images provided. If there isn't an image, draw and colour and create a masterpiece within my masterpiece and make it your own.
Happy creating!

Some content may be triggering.
Read with caution.

Have questions, comments or want to show me your artwork from the book? Email me!

lovely.nightmare.book@gmail.com

TABLE OF CONTENTS

HUSHED WHISPERS...8
CHILDHOOD RULES...9
UNCERTAINTY...10
SILENT SCREAMS...11
BEDTIME RITUAL...12
JOYS OF SUMMER...13
FEAR...14
ESCAPE...15
SISTER...16
BUBBLES...17
OUTBURST...18
FURIOSITY...19
LOVELESS...20
INNOCENCE...21
NO MORE FEAR...22
TERROR...23
TENSION...24
LOOKING GLASS...25
FREEDOM...26
DARTS...27
ELSEWHERE...28
TRAPPED...29
WAR...30
PURSUIT...31
MIND GAMES...32
SILENCE...33
INVISIBLE...34
ISOLATION...35
LOSER...36
TRANQUILITY...37
UNCHANGING...38
OUTCAST...39
DIAMONDS & DIRT...40
SWEET MELODIES...41
UNSUSPECTED...42
TAKE IT AWAY...43
GONE...44
HEAVY...45
DEAD...46
CRITICAL...47
RELEASE...48
BOOM BOOM BOOM...49
DEMONS...50
WHEN...51
UNLIVABLE...52
OLD BROKEN SONG...53
FIGHTING FOR MY PEACE...54
HEALING...55
DANCING IN THE DARK...56

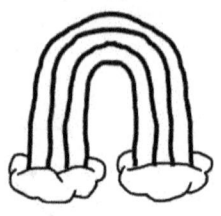

TRY...57
SUBMERGED...58
WITHIN...59
CHOKEHOLD...60
SCARED...61
ONE DAY...62
CRY...63
DID YOU...64
PERFECTLY FINE...65
SUICIDE PLAN...66
YOU FAILED ME...67
BETRAYED...68
OVERWHELMED...69
CONFIDENT...70
NEW LOVE...71
LOVIN' YOU...72
SHINE...73
PARANOIA...74
DAMAGED HEARTS...75
NEED TO HEAL...76
LAST ONE...77
EGGSHELLS....78
DOUBTS...79
WHERE DO WE GO...80
EMPTY SHELL...81
TURPENTINE...82
UNZIPPED...83
COLD LIKE ICE...84
STONE...85
DON'T WALK AWAY...86
RAINBOW...87
FAIL...88
RISE ABOVE...89
DIGNITY...90, 91
STRONG... 92
PANIC...93
ANXIETY...94
ZOMBIE...95
CRASHING...96
TONIGHT...97
HEAVEN...98
IMPLODE...99
CUT...100
REMORSE...101
DEPRESSION...102
CRAVE...103
BUTTERFLY KISSES...104
STOPE & STARE...105
DELIBRATE ACCIDENT...106
HERE...107
NO MORE...108, 109
MY LOVE...110

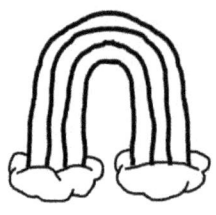
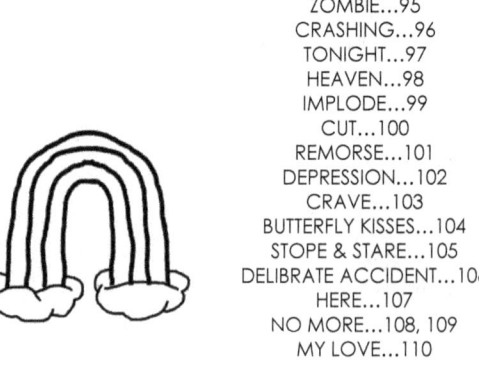

TIRED...111
SPARKS...112
BLAME...113
LILAC TREE...114
LET GO...115
LIES...116
CLARITY...117
LIGHTNING...118
GALAXY...119
HOLD ON...120
FLY...121
ANGEL...122
LOST...123
CHAINS...124
TIME...125
STRONGER...126
RECOVERY...127
THINGS GET BETTER...128
SO RIGHT...129
INSIDE OUT...130
LOVE SONG...131
WARRIOR...132
QUEEN...133
THAT'S OKAY...134
SUMMER AIR...135
STAND...136
FIGHT...137
SHADOW...138
SHAME...139
SMILE...140
LOVE...141
WHEN...142
FOREVER MINE...143
REMEMBER...144
HEART...145
DARK PLACES...146
ACCEPTANCE...147
SUMMER BLOSSOMS...148
BEAUTIFUL...149
BRIGHT...150
DENIAL...151
GRIEF...152
WAVES...153
NEW DAWN...154
VACANCY...155
WILD AND RECKLESS...156
LOVELY NIGHTMARE...157
ABOUT THE AUTHOR...158
DEDICATION...159

Hushed Whispers

My home is a cage
as hushed whispers rip in rage
Accusatory and degrading
I feel so afraid
I take a blanket and cover my head
I'm a refugee on my bed
They think we can't hear them fight
All this anger is trite

Childhood Rules

1. Do as he commands
   or rage will command
2. Ask before you eat
He's the first one to get the meat
3. Don't spill your cup
If you do, irritation will heat up
4. Don't let the dog bark
   His anger will spark

I learned to follow these rules
I didn't want to make him cruel

UNCERTAINTY

Shooting my eyes open wide
all I see is darkness
My heart is beating against my chest
Breath is quick and short
Shaking and afraid
tears spill down my face
Nothing feels real right now
What is happening to me?
Peaceful sleep
disturbed by uncertainty

Silent Screams

Overcome with sudden fright
Instead of fighting I take flight
Dark clouds of fog impair my mind
Trapped; Confined
My mind is being held prisoner
Everything around me is blurred
There's a monster in my head
Unbeknownst, I'm being mislead
Silent screams erupt as tears
Shivers shake with fear
There's something going on inside
I cry until this feeling subsides

Bedtime Ritual

Telling jokes
Eskimo kisses
Laughter all around
You say goodnight
and tuck me in tight
Every night I look forward to this

JOYS OF SUMMER

The aroma of freshly cut grass
accompanies the sound
of birds as they fly past
A gentle breeze
flows over my skin
Closing my eyes
there's peace within
These are the joys of summer

Fear

Do they even know I'm here
watching them as they fight?
Another problem
Another night
My life holds so much fear

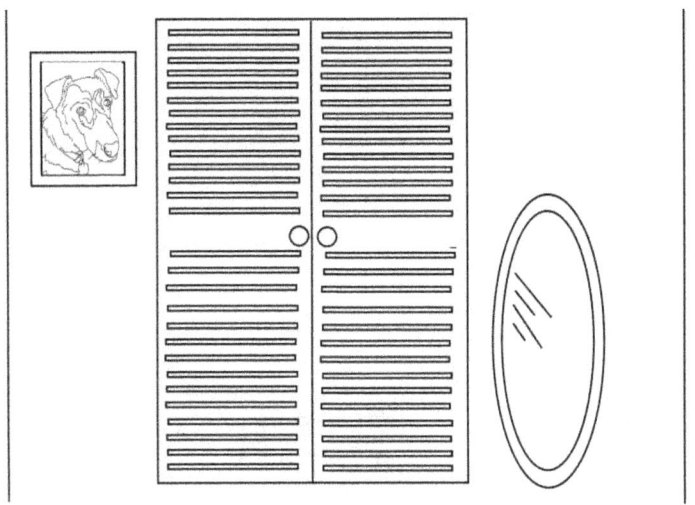

ESCAPE

Alone in my closet
No one can find me here
So much fear emits
I want to disappear
Loud voices
So much distress
Angry choices
makes bigger messes
Darkness hides me
from all my life's debris

LOVELY NIGHTMARE

SISTER

Secrets are whispered in the dark
We hold each other's trust
Laughter emits like echoes
No one else will understand
You're more than my sister
You're my best friend

(Put pictures of your sisters here!)

BUBBLES

Bubbles!
Big ones
Small ones
floating carelessly around
Quick!
Jump in one!
I jump
I land in one
I'm floating above the world
Peaceful
My arms open wide
Spinning 'round and 'round
I float
Leaving the chaos below me

OUTBURST

Peaceful hearts; life is still
Nothing can go wrong
Having fun; laughing loud
Such a joyful sound
Clouds roll in; thunder booms
There is hell to pay
Fear erupts; laughter dies
Anger takes control
Grabs the dog; lifts her up
She yelps and I cry
Throws her down; all the stairs
She cowers in fear
My heart stops; she cries out
Everyone is scared

FURIOSITY

Fearsome screams
Furiosity
Regret drips from my veins
Hiding would have been better
Violence threw that dresser
Hatred made the hole
in the wall
and my heart

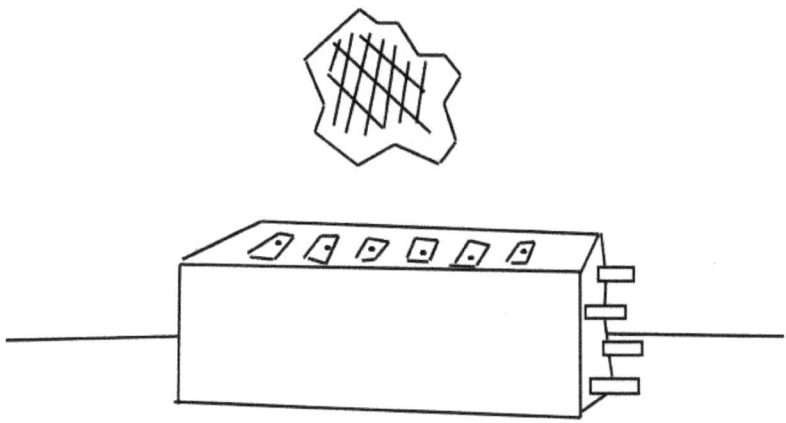

Loveless

Evil spewed from your lips
Names were directed at me
Broken hearted I ran off
I was hurt, couldn't you see?
I was asked what was wrong
as I cried away the pain
I said I didn't feel loved
because you called me a bad name
No emotion was shown to me
I thought she hated me too
Until I heard her yell at him
Being loveless is untrue!

INNOCENCE

A forced friendship I didn't want
An innocent attempt
to raise his confidence
He told me he loved me
I felt slightly uncomfortable
We were only twelve

No More Fear

Secrecy between sisters
A need to release
A need to warn
A life with no more fear
What does that feel like?
No more yelling
No more fighting
No more hiding
No more running
This will all be over soon
But sssshhhh
It's a secret

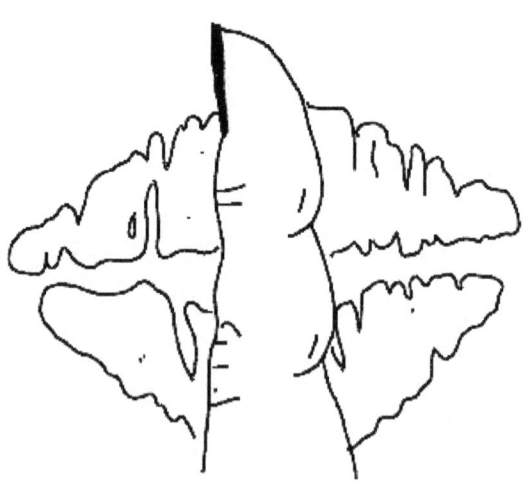

TERROR

Run
Run fast
Don't look back
Just run!
Rigid feet
Shaking legs
Unmovable
Drumming heart
Smashing
Clashing
Erupting visions
Flying objects
He knows the secret
He's coming home
Terror
Run!
Run fast!
Don't look back
Just RUN!

TENSION

New day
New beginnings
Everything is new

Except the tension

It slices through brick
Curdles my insides
Escaping is crucial
I thank God for school
and I leave

Looking Glass

Finally free
No taunting
No whispering
No more forced friendship
No endless fantasies
I could finally live my life
without fear
without his harassment
Free
Until….
Fear rips through my veins
My face is on fire
Sweat drips from every orifice
Panicking
Confused
Hoping it's not true
He's all I can see
Smiling at me
Winking at me
Spinning head
Shaking hands
Screaming heart

He's back

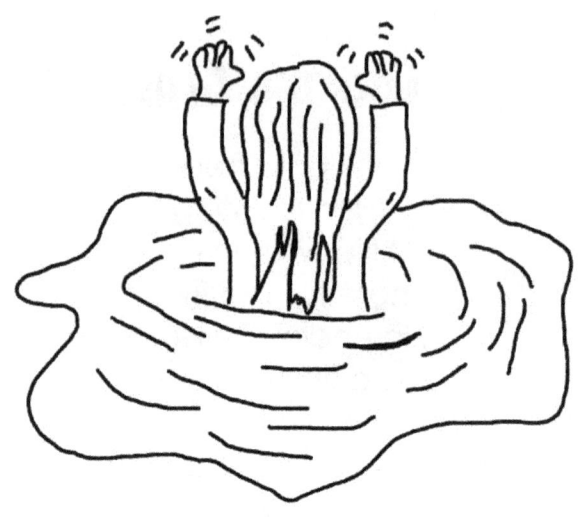

FREEDOM

Anger melts
Sadness sits in a puddle
I'm drowning in so much deceit
This pain needs to be destroyed
Freedom is essential
from the anger
the sadness
from the pain that bounds me
I need to be free from both of you

Darts

You're words stab me like darts
Stop playing games with my heart
I don't know if I can continue
We hold so many issues
Your darts slice at my skin
When can healing begin?
As a parent you need to defuse
I'm done with all the abuse

ELSEWHERE

You've taken this friendship too far
What did my kindness imply to you?
I didn't give you permission to pursue
I don't know how to fight this war
You want your hands all over me
and I don't want them there
My mind is drifting elsewhere
I want to be anywhere but here

TRAPPED

Cornered
like a lion with its prey
Threats
shoot from your lips like bullets
Pornography
shoved in my face
Details
of every sexual act you'd perform
Friendship
is not what we had or what this is
Fear
runs my blood cold
Uncertainty
is how I view my future
A warning from him
"If I catch you after school….

…You're mine."

WAR

You want us to be together
I want you to leave
Uncertainty lies ahead
Breaking apart is paramount
This must end in war

Pursuit

Pursuing me has become his game
His personal cat and mouse
There's no need to explain
how much he was aroused

My heart is thrashing inside my chest
as he chases me down the street
Terror burns in my veins
I feel like a piece of meat

I run as fast as my legs can take me
I don't know where he's hiding
My girlfriend finds him in the alley
Slapping him, he gets a chiding

Tomorrow is another day
when he could track me down
My heart is holding so much dismay
I'm on the brink of a meltdown

Mind Games

Why must you play mind games?
I'm not a child anymore
I know what you're doing
and it won't work
So
I stand my ground
but regret soon fills my heart
My mind is worried about his anger
I cave in
I call him back
He won again
I hate these stupid mind games

SILENCE

Silence fills our new house
There is no more fighting
My closet is no more a refuge
There is only silence
It hangs from the ceiling
And drips onto my head
Sadness is my new companion
Loneliness decided to walk with me
I love the silence
but I also hate it

INVISIBLE

Clink
Clank
Clunk
Pennies hit the back of my head
An empty pop can flies past
Tears erupt; don't let them show
Defeated
Embarrassed
Angry
Laughter at my expense
The movie plays; teacher sleeps
I wish I could be invisible

ISOLATION

I sit in my room; alone
Omnious clouds; above my head
Loneliness; eating my soul
Attention; I hate it
The staring
The judgment
The awkwardness
Isolation; my paradise
Bullying; not here
Nothing can reach me here

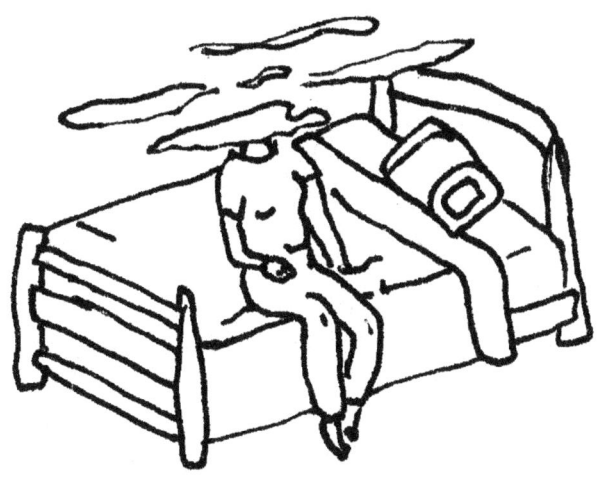

LOSER

His words stab me
Humiliation makes me want to die
He picks on me so all could see
that he can make me cry
and it works
I hate him with passion
as my face feels like flames
For once I want to win
this stupid teenage game
But I lose
Every
Single
Time
I'm such a loser

TRANQUILITY

Stars are shining
The moon is bright
There's a peaceful breeze tonight
I close my eyes
Breathe in the air
releasing all I can't bare
Strength flows
silencing all thoughts
For a moment
I'm no longer distraught

Unchanging

New school year
New school
New friends
New house
New brothers
New dad
Same sadness

Outcast

I'm sitting alone
watching people pass me by
No one sits or talks to me
and I want nothing but to cry
My heart feels so heavy
My thoughts you can't see
My self-esteem is falling fast
for I am an outcast
Walking in the hallway
I hear laughter from all sides
I feel like I'm being judged
and want nothing but to hide
My heart feels so heavy
My tears you can't see
My self-esteem is falling fast
for I am an outcast

DIAMONDS & DIRT

Fading sleep
Rescue fast
Falling pieces
Let's hope I last
Diamonds and dirt
lay on the floor
I don't want to hurt
and feel so insecure
Someone take my tears
Please steal my pain
Tell me I'll be alright
Diamonds and dirt
Lay on the floor
I don't want to hurt anymore

Sweet Melodies

Sweet melodies of music divine
fill my ears with a voice so fine
Happiness settles within my heart
forcing the anger to depart
No more hatred and no more tears
This voice releases all my fears
Angel in disguise
you've saved my life
You've held me up in times of strife
The words you sing
connect with me
in years past and in years to come
Please
don't stop making sweet sounds
You've saved me from me
I've been found

UNSUSPECTED

I haven't seen your face for a while
and I'm glad
As you now stand in front of me
I can't breathe
Can't think
Just feel
Afraid
Fearful
Dirty
Broken
Our eyes connect
I want nothing more than to vomit

Take It Away

Erase the pain
Take it away
The agony can make anyone
feel insane!
I need to use all I know
so I can survive this war
Erase the pain
Take it away
Hearts are full of disdain
Take it all away

GONE

You left me feeling angry
when you took your life away
I was jealous that you got to leave
and I was left to stay
I still want to be like you
I want to be gone
Gone
Gone

Heavy

My soul is heavy
and no one seems to know
They never will
unless I let it show

Dead

Somebody needs to see
the hurt inside of me
I just want to disappear
The yearning is so severe
Misery spills from my pores
I'm done fighting this war
As my brain screams
"You're better off dead
Dead
DEAD"

CRITICAL

Hurting myself is frequent
It's one of my many secrets
Visions of death eat my mind
I'm tired of being so confined
I need assistance
I hate my existence
I think I'm mentally ill
Telling someone is critical

RELEASE

Opening my heart
Spilling my emotions
Everything spews out
Stress is released
The mess in my head dissipates
My teacher is there
Helping me sort life out

Boom Boom Boom

Singin' in the rain
Dancin' in the street
My joy is so great
Nothing can compete
So profound is this feeling
beating in my chest
This life has been blessed
Love is singing in my heart
Dance to the beat
of the boom boom boom
My smile is radiant
My eyes so bright
Let's have a wonderful night

DEMONS

They're in your head
They're all around
These demons
can easily pull you down

When

Releasing all that's within
stopped me from cutting my skin
But much to my chagrin
depression comes back for the win
When can healing begin?

UNLIVABLE

Dig me out and lift me up
My soul is drowning
The need for pain
is much too high
The shame is paralyzing
This life is unlivable

OLD BROKEN SONG

Tell me everything will be alright
that I will not die tonight
Tell me to hold on
Tell me to fight
Give me your hand
to hold on tight
My heart has been aching
way too long
I can't stop singing
this old broken song
There's no peace in my soul
only a big black hole
I need reassurance
that one day I'll feel whole
My heart has been aching
for way too long
I can't keep singing
this old broken song

Fighting For My Peace

Fight for peace
Battle through
Take up the shield
Protect yourself
Willpower is strong
Conquer
Rise to the top
Fighting for my peace

HEALING

Cuts on my skin
proves nothing has changed
Someone else has to help me
Professional help needs to begin
so I write my secrets on paper
for my mother to see
Freedom flows from within
Counseling is scheduled
Healing can begin

Dancing In The Dark

Taking on a new beginning
Dancing my cares away
With my hands in the air
and my body with the beat
Dancing my cares away
Dancing in the dark

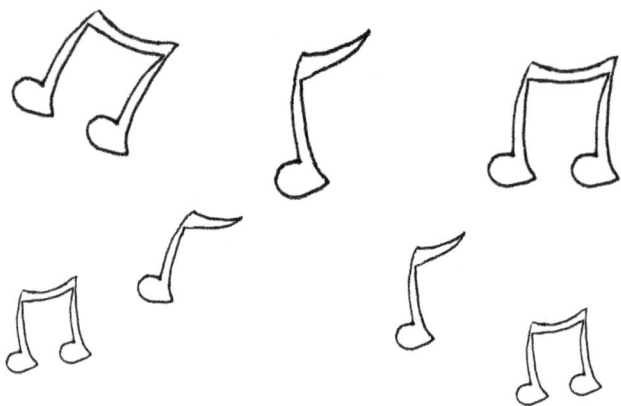

TRY

A room full of invisible trauma
Secrets paint the walls
Unseen sorrow fills the sofa
Broken hearts braid the carpet
The light above casts down hope
Thoughts of death depart
The woman across from me smiles
I want to give healing a try

SUBMERGED

For once my mind is silent
A new emotion emerges
My thoughts aren't violent
Is my melancholy submerged?

WITHIN

Like a spy in the night
misery eats at my mind
There's so much anguish
deep within my soul
Can't seem to save myself
from the pain it causes within
A never ending grief
My mind is being deceived
Can't seem to save myself
from the pain it causes within

Chokehold

Depression
has my heart in a chokehold
The grip I can't escape
Running; screaming; crying
Can't break the chains
Need it; want it; crave it
Addicted to the pain
Depression
has my heart in a chokehold
The grip I can't escape
These feelings have a way
of strangling me until I'm weak

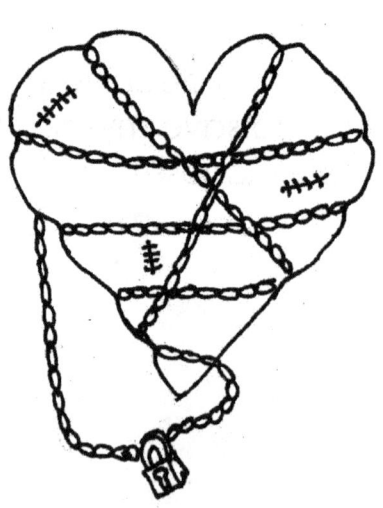

SCARED

Alone again in my room
Aren't you worried?
Aren't you scared?
I'm growing up way too fast
Aren't you worried?
Aren't you scared?
Inside I hurt, inside I cry
Aren't you worried?
Aren't you scared?
Why don't you ask me?
What's on your mind?
Why do you keep it inside?
Are you worried too?
I'm scared just like you

One Day

Poetry puts words to pain
Sorts out the feelings
Carries the soul
above the cloud of depression
making everything
for the moment
worth it
Song lyrics free the soul
so you can see what lies below
Music plays
Tears fall
"Everything will be okay"
they sing
Everything **will** be okay

One day

CRY

Cry for the love
Cry for the hate
Cry the pain
it makes me insane
Cry for the world
and cry for you too
Cry for depression
I'm sure it's eating you too

DID YOU

All I needed was your affection
just a little emotional attention
but the more I was ignored
the deeper my sadness soared
Did you ever love me?
Did you ever care?
I felt neglected and rejected
and painfully disconnected
My words felt invisible
My presence inadmissible
Did you ever love me?
Did you ever care?
Why did you always criticize?
What I needed most
was for you to empathize
All I needed was your affection
just a little emotional attention
but the more I was ignored
the deeper my sadness soared
Did you ever love me?
Did you ever care?

Perfectly Fine

I'm crying but I'm fine
Perfectly fine
I'm so angry but I'm fine
Perfectly fine
I want to see blood
but I'm fine
I'M FINE
Perfectly fine
Stop asking me how I'm doing
I'm fine
Perfectly fine
I close my eyes
and I see darkness
For a moment
everything is fine
Perfectly fine

Suicide Plan

Home alone
Living in a danger zone
No hope
Can't cope
Suicide
I need to try
Tears
showing my fears
Pills
A sadistic thrill
Phone chimes
This is not the time!
I answer
My friends confer
They arrive
I stay alive

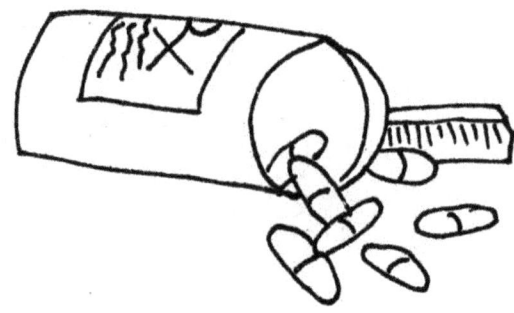

You Failed Me

Lost my grip
Falling fast
Too much is going on
I reach out
I need help
But she says I'm crazy
Hope dies out
I hate life
She just made things worse
Just listen!
Help me please!
She just keeps yelling
I'm bawling
She hangs up
Now I hate you too

BETRAYED

Go away
Don't come back
Your love I lack
Stick a needle in my eye
You stabbed me in the back

OVERWHELMED

Overwhelmed with life's events
Underwhelmed for life
Failed friendships
Lost confidants
Ankle sprain
Searing pain
Graduation
Now what's next?
Get a job; it's demanded
Go to school; no help provided
Dissociation at its best
I am so overwhelmed

Confident

Making progress is slow
I entered counseling long ago
Talk therapy is God sent
I feel more confident

New Love

Excitement floods my veins
This new love has much to gain
The world is bright tonight
Look me in the eyes all night
I want to drink you up

LOVIN' YOU

I'm lovin' how you watch me eat
watch me sleep
watch me while I watch TV
I'm lovin' how you smile to yourself
every time I touch you
look at you
look at you, lookin' at me
I'm lovin' all the things you say
I'm lovin' all the things you do
Hey baby
I really do love you

SHINE

Your face is close to mine
Our fingers lovingly intertwine
My heart feels light
Our love ignites
This life is ours to shine
We'll say "I do"
and "I love you"
and pray we'll be alright
This life is ours
and like the stars
this life is ours to shine

PARANOIA

Don't think about it
Ignore it
The sky gets dark
The fear sets in
This familiar paranoia
Tears run down my face
Sadness sneaks in
Anger erupts
I need to scream
I need to escape
This familiar paranoia

Damaged Hearts

Unbearable damaged hearts
Twist and turn within our chests
this is love gone wrong

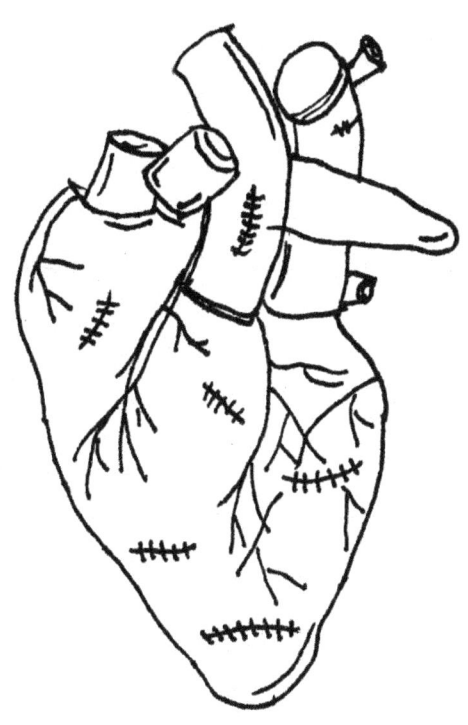

Need To Heal

The day you walked out the door
is the day my heart
smashed on the floor
Too many thoughts
Too many feelings
so I fight all day
and cry the whole way
Need to heal
but I can barely feel
I wish for sleep
but in you creep
Tossing and turning
I crave your return
I dream of love
Of me
Of us
so I fight all day
and cry the whole way
Need to heal
but I can barely feel

Last One

I was the last one to hold you
talk to you
and tell you that I loved you
I was the last one
who told you to go
that you would be okay
I was the last one to kiss you
touch you
have a special moment with you
I know you felt my love
and at that moment
I know you loved me too

EGGSHELLS

Life is not meant to be spent
walking on eggshells
not knowing what will happen
if you crack
The words that are spoken
The actions that are pursued
will never be good enough for you
I'm walking on eggshells
You've caused so much damage
I can't spend my life
walking on eggshells
I am no longer your detainee
You will never be
good enough for me

Doubts

All these doubts
are making me insane?
All this pain
is no fun and games
My eyes are welling up
My heart; it feels dead
So many doubts
floating in my head

LOVELY NIGHTMARE

Where Do We Go?

Where do we go from here?
Our relationship holds fear
We used to be tight
but now we only fight
My heart is bruised
from your hurtful words
There's no way to understand
Your thoughts are absurd
Our love is dying
Where do we go from here?

Empty Shell

I'm an empty shell of a woman
who's searching for stability
because of infertility
Constant reminders are everywhere
of one thing I cannot attain
I'm trying to find some ground
My earth is trembling at the core
My mind is lost, I can't be found
I'm an empty shell of a woman
who's searching for stability
because of infertility

TURPENTINE

You're just like turpentine
stripping me of my colours
You're dulling my shine
I'm naked around you
with nothing left to show

Unzipped

His words are thrown like grenades
Another war in my head invades
The hopelessness I feel is intense
Nothing is making sense
So I run for the door
I don't want to be alive anymore
I scream and I cry
As I tell him I want to die
Hatred for life spills from my lips
The truth is unzipped

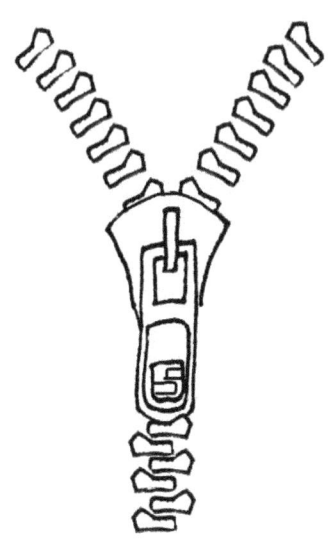

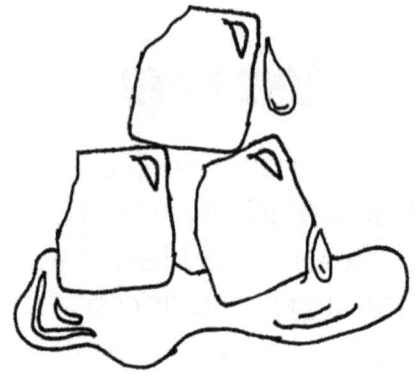

Cold Like Ice

Broken spirit
Troubled heart
Sometimes this life
I want to depart
Confused mind
Lonely soul
Buried
in a deep black hole
Help me
Dig me out
Buried
in all these doubts
Here I lay
cold like ice

STONE

I try to speak but I can't
I try to tell you how I feel
Can't seem to find the words inside
to express the sadness I conceal
So
I cry until my heart feels lightened
I wonder where you are
Am I in this fight alone?
My heart ain't made of stone
I weep away all my burdens
Shake away the doubt
The silence swallows me up whole
I can't contain the buildup no more
So
I cry until my heart feels lightened
I wonder where you are
Am I in this fight alone?
My heart ain't made of stone
I weep away all my burdens
Shake away the doubt
Am I in this fight alone?
My heart ain't made of stone

Don't Walk Away

Please don't ever walk away
In my heart you will stay
Love makes the world go round
in a surprisingly pleasant sound
I sit and cry
wishing you're by my side
I need you
Don't walk away

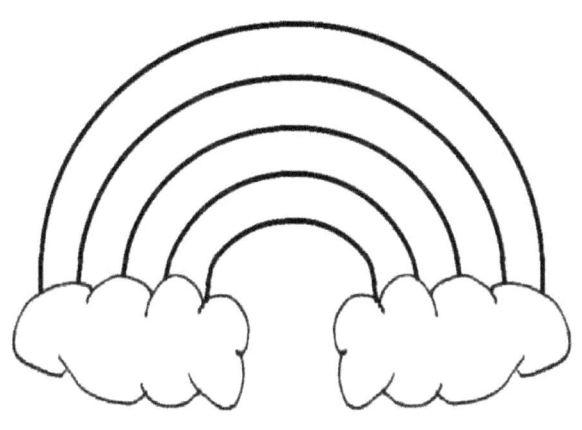

Rainbow

Our love for each other
grows and grows
and like the river it gently flows
You are my rainbow shining bright
giving me hope
and helping me fight
Keep lighting my darkness
and shining my way
I love you more than words can say

FAIL

You had one obligation
But you failed
I was brought up to doubt myself
Hate myself
Be a soul with low esteem
A person who struggles

Every

Single

Day

RISE ABOVE

Hard life
Too many trials
Some days
you need to cry for a while
Can't stop now
Breathe out
Look all around
You're not the only one
who's been knocked down
Have courage to keep going
Don't forget to have some fun
Soar towards the love
Float above the negativity
Rise Above

DIGNITY

Like a bird in flight I'm flying away
I'll soar above the clouds while I survey
I'll watch you in your misery
I'll wish away your pain
but know that how you've treated me
has filled me with disdain
You just keep on damaging
My heart keeps on bruising
and nothing can ever be the same
You're vindictive and malicious
You're cunning and pernicious
Your dignity you need to reclaim
My heart aches in pain so I wordlessly cry
as you beat me with words
I want to deny
You've sunken too deep
in your personal woes
And now you attack those
who are happy and composed
You've had a hard life, I know this is true
but your compassion and respect
need to make a debut
Your class act is failing
and starting to demise
You need to watch your words
and what they apprise

I can sense all your strife
and emotional pain
as your lips spew out venom
like a snake in disdain
I tried to reach out to make things okay
but you're pushing me over
you're blowing me away
You just keep on damaging
My heart keeps on bruising
and nothing can ever be the same
You're vindictive and malicious
You're cunning and pernicious
Your dignity you need to reclaim

STRONG

I love you today
I love you right now
These feelings will go on
My heart is beating strong

Panic

Frustration explodes
within my veins
My whole body
is bound by chains
This anxiety is hell
There's no way out
I'm overwhelmed
Everything around me
is so peculiar
Every second is a war
Screams come from within
When can the peace begin?
Loosen the chains of death
There's so much fear
I'm losing my breath!

ANXIETY

Overbearing hopelessness
Shallow breath
Wide eyes
Uncontrollable tears
Scorching hatred
Debilitating depression
Need to die

ZOMBIE

There's a secret side
which no one should see
A zombie
unleashed by rage
Too far gone, disengaged
A zombie
A monster that's risen
Racing heart
Sweaty palms
Raging temper
Bloodshot eyes
A zombie
The monster inside
is no more imprisoned

Crashing

My world is crashing down
whenever I turn around
Tomorrow may be another day
but right now is now
There's too many emotions
Unsure of what to feel
My world is crashing down

Tonight

Earthly battles
tear me down
makes me cry
and makes me drown
Like a warrior
I will fight
It'll only make me
stronger tonight

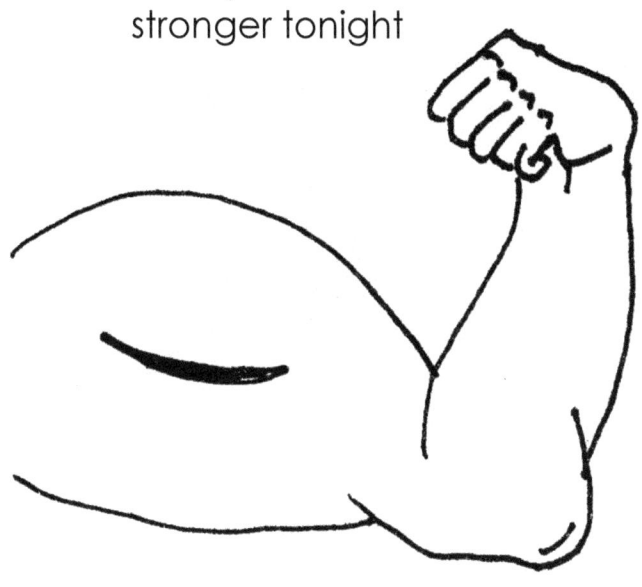

LOVELY NIGHTMARE

Heaven

I've fallen from the sky
and landed in your arms
Looking around
with you holding me tight
I always think to myself
"How did I get so lucky?"
This feels just like heaven

IMPLODE

I climb one mountain
to fall in an emotional tailspin
Happiness always crumbles
leaving me to stumble
Why is this life
filled with so much strife?
I need a way to release
so I can feel at peace
With no talk therapy
I can't feel free
Anger about life boils
My life is so embroiled!
I'm going to implode
My faith in life is eroding

CUT

There's a whisper deep inside
There's nowhere to hide

"Just once"
"That's all it will take"
"You deserve it"
"No one will know"
"It will feel so good"

So I obey
I pick up my weapon
and I cut
again
and again
and again
(Cut this page instead of your skin)

KRYSTAL GRAY

Remorse

Remorse drips like blood
that spilled from inside
A symbol of struggle
An attempt to feel better

Depression

Damn ugly voice
Emitting lies into my brain
Pretending I'm worthless
Relentlessly
Endlessly
Saying I'm insignificant
Shutting it out seems hopeless
Imposing it's lies
Overwhelming the senses
Numbing my brain

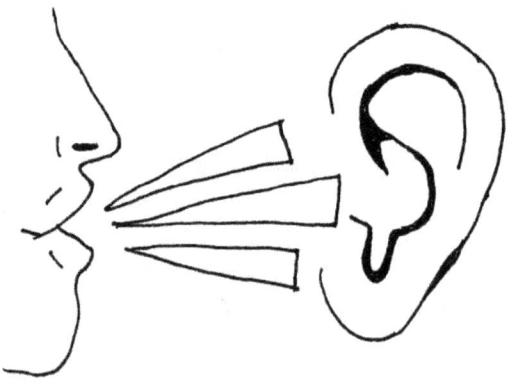

CRAVE

The sensation hits
The visual is appealing
The action is healing
Day by day it's needed
Yearning
Craving
Can't live without it
Irresistible
Tempting
Alluring
Denying the craving is beneficial
but I can't

Butterfly Kisses

We're living in a love story
with butterfly kisses
You are my Mr.
and I am your Mrs.
We are in love
forever and beyond
With every sunset
our hearts grow a stronger bond
I'd give anything for you
You're the one I'll always run to
You are my Mr.
and I am your Mrs.
We are living in a love story
with butterfly kisses

STOP & STARE

My heart is shattered
on the floor
Jagged pieces on the ground
My tears are cold
against my skin
Icy pellets feel like pins
The world has stopped
for me to stare
I fall to the floor
like levity's not there
Here I lay with pieces of heart
I need to cry to let it out
but my veins are wide
torn open in fear
Fatigue dried up all my tears
As time passes by
the numbness fades
My tears are free to cascade
My heart is no longer
on the floor
I cry tears no more
The world goes on unaware
and all I can do is stop and stare

DELIBERATE ACCIDENT

The urge is strong
The impulse
bleeds into my thoughts
Tears stream down
I didn't mean for this to happen;
a deliberate accident
The sadness ate my heart away
My eyes close tight
with deep intent
I didn't mean for this to happen;
a deliberate accident
There was so much unhappiness
I didn't mean for this to happen;
a deliberate accident

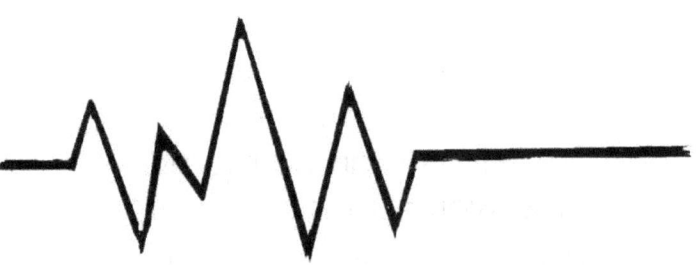

Here

Sometimes life seems so unfair
from all the trials that cause despair
You've been through a lot
and held on strong
Hopefully your hardships won't last for long
Just know that I'm here
I won't disappear
You can count on me
You spend your nights alone
crying tears of sadness
feeling so disowned
Your world is unstable under your feet
Don't fall into weakness and cry defeat
Just know that I'm here
I won't disappear
You can count on me
Here's some hope
Have my faith
and take my love too
Put it in a tight sealed jar
and remember
I'll endlessly love you
Just know that I'm here
I won't disappear
You can count on me

No More

You're not needed anymore
Stop this foolish war
There's holes in my heart
and tears in my eyes
There's no way to forget all your lies
Visions of words remain in my head
of every mean thing
that you've ever said
Now my heart is strong
All along you were wrong
Your actions hurt like stones
Your words cut like knives
There's no more blood on the floor
You're not going to
affect me anymore
Moving forward, moving on
This abuse
has been going on too long
Self-respect
has me leaving you behind
You're now just a memory
in the back of my mind
but there's still holes in my heart

KRYSTAL GRAY

and tears in my eyes
There's no way
I can forget all of your lies
Visions of words remain in my head
of every mean thing
that you've ever said
Now that my tenacity
has helped me grow strong
My brain realizes
all along you were wrong

(Write down all your lies in her head)

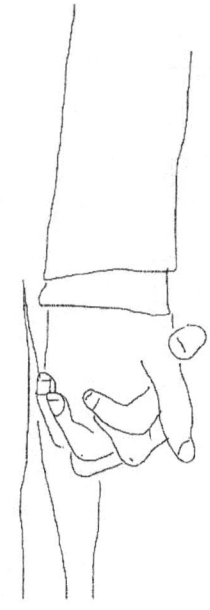

My Love

I've got your back
and you've got mine
My love for you
will always shine
Our bond is strong
Nothing can compare
My love for you
will always be there

TIRED

Can't smile anymore
Can't find reasons
Too many thoughts
Too big of a war
Crumbling from within
Happiness is a lie
I've tried but now I'm tired

SPARKS

Respect is shown in your gaze
Her smile shows admiration
when you kiss each other on the lips
Sparks ignite
Love takes flight

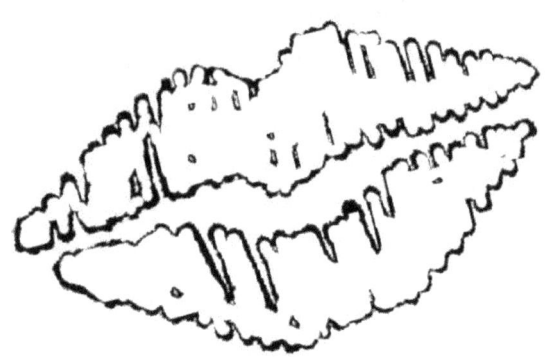

BLAME

Thoughts swirl in my mind
Ending it all has me in a bind
Opening my eyes wide
screams erupt from inside
My mind keeps playing games
I need to find who's to blame
I'm constantly fighting
Fighting to keep
my strength alive
Fighting not to cut
my skin open wide
I think I'm the one to blame

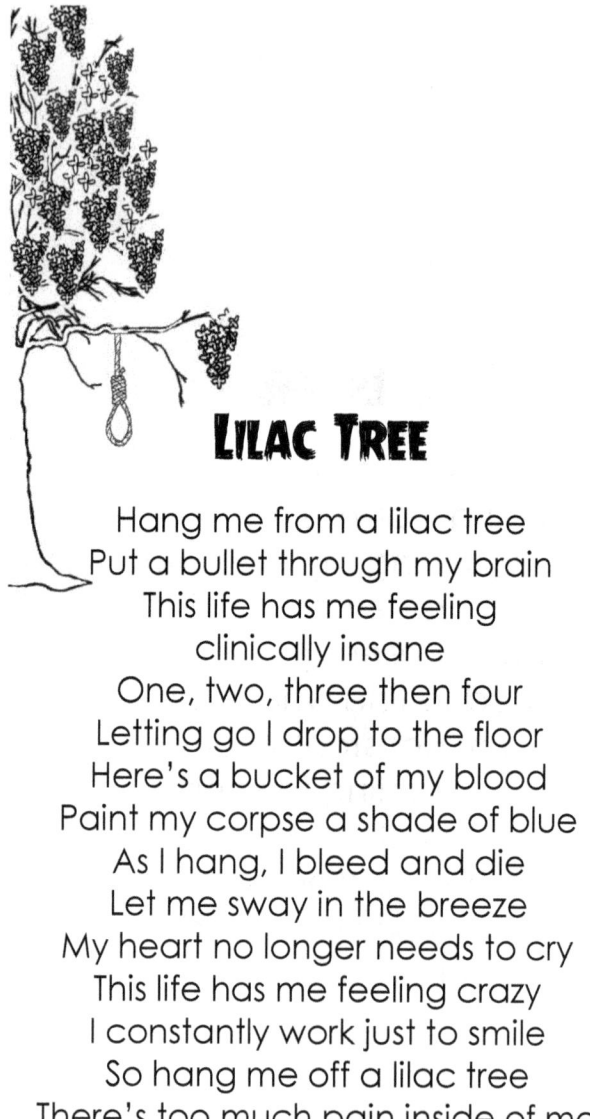

LILAC TREE

Hang me from a lilac tree
Put a bullet through my brain
This life has me feeling
clinically insane
One, two, three then four
Letting go I drop to the floor
Here's a bucket of my blood
Paint my corpse a shade of blue
As I hang, I bleed and die
Let me sway in the breeze
My heart no longer needs to cry
This life has me feeling crazy
I constantly work just to smile
So hang me off a lilac tree
There's too much pain inside of me

Let Go

Let your worries float away
Watch them dissolve in the air
Everything will be okay one day
Let your fears go

(Write your worries in the clouds)

LIES

I drank up all of your filthy lies
where you said you loved me
you'd die for me
always be there for me
You poured cold liquid
into big metal cup
and like an idiot
I drank up all of your lies

CLARITY

Excitement erupts for the day
There's good in everything
Let's pray this feeling stays
One mishap and it could all fall

Down

Down

Down

When the mind isn't a war zone
there's a possibility to sink
but when the mind is clear
and free from the voices within
clarity is the lottery
and you have just won

LOVELY NIGHTMARE

Lightning

You're stronger than you think
You're capable of anything
Push through the crowd
Make lots of sound
Bright like lightning
Loud like thunder

GALAXY

Our love was made from stardust
extracted from the galaxy
A spoonful of trust
A dash of loyalty
There's more to us than lust

Hold On

Round and round
this big world spins
Don't let all the negativity in!
Bad things happen
and we may cry
but happiness can make you fly
Take a minute to redirect
Hold on to the hope
that's inside of your heart
Don't worry if you fall apart
Hold on to the love
that sings to your soul
You own the keys
Your life is in your control
Hold onto the laughter
Hold onto the joy
Don't let sadness be a decoy
Hold onto the happiness
I know is within
Positivity is the only thing
that will help you win
Round and round
this big world spins
Don't let all the negativity in!

Fly

Life is complicated;
I'm not going to lie
Stop wishing you were dead
And instead, learn to fly

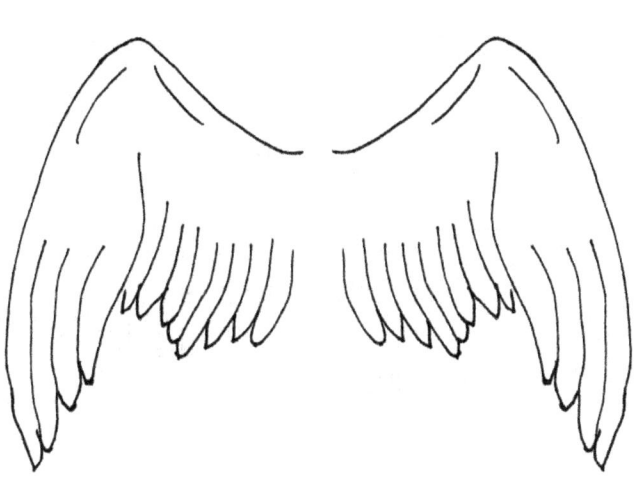

ANGEL

Her spirit moves on
as it sadly leaves
My heart cries out as I grieve
She called me her angel;
her love for me shined
but now she's also mine

Lost

Like a ticking clock, I feel it
My mind is changing
My thoughts are slowing down
bit by bit
Before I realize what's happening
I've lost it
All joy
All happiness
All motivation
Gone
And now I'm just sitting here
staring into nowhere
My emotions are numb
There's not even fear
I'm empty with a blank stare
because I've lost it
All joy
All happiness
All motivation
Gone

CHAINS

Standing my ground
Need some air; going to drown
Bound
Something cracked within
Found
Breaking free
I'm destroying the chains
that are binding me

# Time

Time and time again
you tell me important things
Over and over
replayed in different words
Different forms
Different tones of voice
Time and time again
you reassure me
Prompting me
you tell me I'm strong and resilient
A fighter
Time and time again
the need to talk to you is high
or just be in your presence
because it sooths me
calms me
Time and time again
my heart feels soothed
this is my safe place
A place of peace
A place of understanding
A place of truth

STRONGER

Stay Strong
Through it all
Remember crying isn't wrong
Open your life
Neglect the strife
Gratitude enhances attitude
Everything affects your mood
Remember where you belong

RECOVERY

Is recovery possible
when depression and anxiety
are right behind me
waiting
anticipating
when it can jump out
and eat me whole?

Things Get Better

Things get better
with each passing day
Fulfilment takes effort
Positivity takes time
Determination is the key
Fight the fight
Things get better

So Right

Sippin' soda pop in the front yard
Everything's pretty chill
There's something in the air tonight
and everything feels so right
Grab my hand and hold my waist
Sway my body to the beat
Tonight is gonna be a great night
Everything feel so right
Fireworks pop overhead
There's nowhere I'd rather be
Happiness is in my sight
Everything feels so right

Inside Out

Life has a way
of pulling us down
making us drown
Stand up for the fight
and you will see
so much glee
feeling free
Joy is not having
a level of degree
We are warriors
Fighters who defend
when sadness attends
and anxiety suspends
We know who we are
and what we're about
Confidence, let's shout
Happiness, no doubt
Let's turn ourselves
Inside out

LOVE SONG

There isn't a love song quite like mine
As affectionate
as wonderfully divine
so crafted into something...
Perfection
Passion
Desire

Warrior

Underneath, I am a warrior
I know I'll stand up tall again
I'll shield my heart
from all the pain
I'm never going down again!
Underneath, I am a warrior
I'll extract my sword
to defend my soul
Through life's battles
I'll stand my ground
I am a warrior
I am never going down

Queen

You are worthy of love
Look in the mirror
Hold your head high
Don't forget
Put on your crown
Reign in happiness
You are a queen

That's Okay

Life with mental illness isn't easy
So much is going on
that others cannot see
When I smile
am I telling you a lie?
Saying that I'm glad
when in reality I'm feeling sad?
People with mental illness
can be happy too
despite all the wild animals
living in our zoo
but sometimes we slip
sometimes we slide
and experience an episode
where we do nothing but cry
And that's okay
Today is one day
and tomorrow is another
With the help from friends
we can get through this together
So next time you're sad
or feeling like you've slipped
remember that life is a journey
and everybody trips

SUMMER AIR

Feeling the hot summer air anew
please hold me close for I love you
In the heat of the night
our lips will linger
Our hearts beat wildly
through our entwined fingers
Chest to chest and face to face
I'm here right now in your embrace
The touch of your fingers against my skin;
it draws my breath deep within
My love for you will always grow
I hope my actions let it show
Our sweet memories reside in me
More will come I guarantee
Knowing you
has made my life worthwhile
You always seem to make me smile
Feeling the hot summer air anew
our memories come back
like a debut
and if there was one thing
I had to say
It would be
"my love for you grows everyday"

STAND

Stand tall
Rise above
Stay strong
Fight the war
Realize what you stand for
Happiness can be yours
Reach out
Don't resign
Hold onto the light
Stay strong
Fight this war
Realize what you stand for

FIGHT

Everything will work out
Dry your tears
Put the sadness away
Before you can see the light
the darkness you have to fight

SHADOW

Mental illness is a shadow
always there
always lurking
Use your shadow to reach out
to shout
to tell people what living
with mental illness
is really about
It's not just sad days
laying in bed
thinking about death
and feeling utter dread
It can be a tool to help others
who are feeling the same thing
Know that you are not alone;
A lot of people have shadows
When you're feeling strong enough
let your shadow aid others
to find that shining light

Shame

The woman inside me
is no longer the same
Hearts have been broken
trust has been lost
Suddenly my emotions
are as cold as frost
Teardrops are falling
from my eyes
There were so many
unspoken lies
All I'm left with is shame

LOVELY NIGHTMARE

Smile

When you're feeling down
lift your head and smile
It will be hard at first
It might take a while
A smile can help you cope
A smile can mend your day
A smile can bring you hope

Love

Laughter erupts from our lips
Our love is like a rose
Vivid memories of us will reside
Everyday our love enfolds

When

When hearts collide
hate is the guide
and trust is denied
When fear ignites
nothing feels alright
and I'm in a haze of fright
When sadness erupts
life as you know it sucks
and you feel corrupt
When happiness flows
everyone knows
and nothing creates woes
Life is full of emotion
It demands devotion
You are the guide
You choose the motion

Forever Mine

Illuminated by candle light
your face is close to mine
Memories flood my senses
of all the times we've shared
We started off young
and now we are older
You are forever mine

REMEMBER

Cruisin' with the windows down
Music in our ears
An open road outside of town
Let's remember this for years
The world can be a wonderful place
with smiles from passersby
glued to their face
Let's remember when I didn't cry

Heart

My heart is not like others
The emotions are deeper
stronger
harder
Loving everyone comes freely
easily
effortlessly
Internalizing that love is needed
so self-love can succeed

Dark Places

Another night of crying
sitting in the dark
wondering how and when
happiness can embark

Hide me from the dark places
that take up refuge in my head
Lies filter through the cracks
telling me I'm better off dead

ACCEPTANCE

Getting out of bed is hard today
My depression needs to go away
Heaviness fills my body
The mental torment is beastly
Fog impairs my mind
Frustration is assigned
Clarity makes a debut
This is a trial I'll always go through
I know that the storm will clear
My heart holds no more fear
So I sit in it
Accept it
Then I fight
At the end of this tunnel
I know there is light

LOVELY NIGHTMARE

Summer Blossoms

Our love blooms daily
And just like the summer blossoms
we'll keep growing strong

Beautiful

You are beautiful
no matter what
You are beautiful
despite the size of your butt
You are beautiful
even if you don't like
the size of your gut
You are beautiful
Climb out of the rut
that tells you you're not
In spite of your size
despite your race
You
Are
Beautiful

BRIGHT

Stars cannot shine without darkness
so look through all your difficulties
Your life isn't one big mess
this is the day you need to seize
You're bright like a star
You'll go far
Be happy for those bad days
Struggles are nothing but a phase

DENIAL

A hole digs into my heart
where your love used to gather
I still smile but I feel empty
I've lost a part of me

Tears chisel down my face
where laughter used to erupt
I'm still breathing but slowly
I don't want this to be my reality

GRIEF

Grief
ripping apart my insides
distorting my reality
I'm in total disbelief

WAVES

Like the ocean
my grief comes in waves
The emotions ebb and flow
as I struggle to realize
it's your time to go
My waves will be calm
until a storm arrives
then my tears create a tsunami
until there is nothing left inside
No map, no direction of where to go
I am lost at sea
This grief needs room to be
Like the ocean
my grief comes in waves
High tide and low tide
I'm riding these waves
because you died

New Dawn

I stumbled and I fell
I thought I lived in hell
I crawled my way out
Now I want to shout:
I'm happy and feel cheer
My mind feels so clear
I notice all that I have
I decided to be glad
I want to feel clarity
I want to feel prosperity
I need this to be
my new dawn

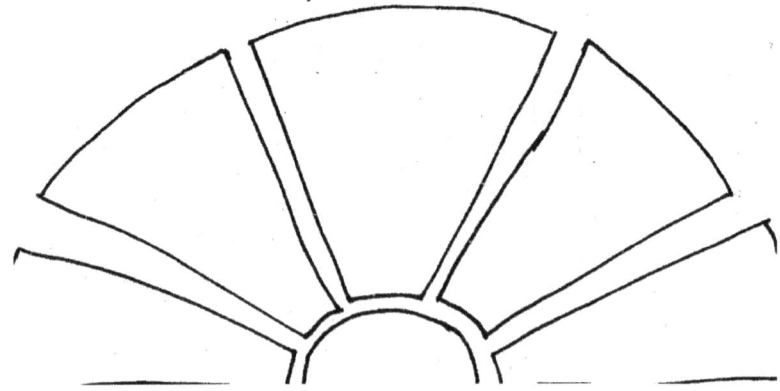

VACANCY

There's a vacancy in my life
because you didn't survive
Twelve years and it soared by
and now I do nothing but cry
My heart is vacant of your presence
and in its place is intense sorrow
May your spirit be at peace
but know that my love will never cease
I will never say goodbye
because in my heart you will stay

WILD AND RECKLESS

Wild and reckless you blasted into my heart
I can't believe it was your time to depart
So young, so carefree
Loving you brought me so much glee
Without warning you were taken
into heaven leaving me with depression
Wild and reckless
was the name of your game
My life will never be the same

Lovely Nightmare

Look at my life and what it's become;
I'm a beautiful mess who has come undone
The world all around
has crashed from within
but I always stand up and fight for the win
The road may be long and tears I will shed
My heart knows
I will have moments of dread
That's when my thoughts swirl into place
and I know I'll be fine through God's grace
So when I'm going through trials and despair
I brainstorm words
to create a lovely nightmare
The words create a lullaby to my ears
as they hold my emotions
and express my fears
The content may be dark
but some find it lovely
the way my words create
an emotional discovery
Look at me and who I've become
I'm beautifully awkward
and I feel like I've won
When I'm going through trials
and deep despair
I brainstorm words
that create a lovely nightmare

ABOUT THE AUTHOR

Krystal grew up in Southern Alberta
but resides in Ontario with her husband
and her black cat, Onyx. While writing this
book she mourns the sudden loss of her
two cats, Spyke and Simba.

Writing has always been Krystal's passion.
At the age of 15 Krystal wrote her first
poem and learned that writing is a great
outlet while dealing with mental illness.

Krystal wants to pass on the healing of
poetry to help others and to help people
know they are not alone and there **IS** hope
for a better future.

Dedication

This book is dedicated to my
Uncle Darren who created the
illustrations for the front
and back cover.
He passed away at the age
of 47 on November 8th, 2017 while
this book was still in editing.

May you finally be at peace.
I love you.

www.ingramcontent.com/pod-product-compliance
Lightning Source LLC
Chambersburg PA
CBHW060156050426
42446CB00013B/2858